Who lives in a rainforest?

Rainforests are home to millions of animals and plants. People live there too. A place that is home to lots of animals and plants is called a habitat. Rainforests are very special habitats.

Draw
What kind of habitat do you live in? Draw a picture of it and colour it in.

which lizard can bark?

There are not many dogs in the jungle, but there are lizards that bark! They are called tokay geckos. Their bark sounds like 'to-kay, to-kay'. These lizards climb trees and hunt bugs at night.

Macaws

Big mouth

Potoos are jungle birds that eat insects at night. They have big, gaping mouths and swallow their food whole.

why do parrots talk?

Parrots talk for the same reason we do — they need to tell each other things. When most parrots talk they twitter, screech and squawk. Some sounds are a warning. They tell other parrots that danger may be nearby.

Why do toucans have big bills?

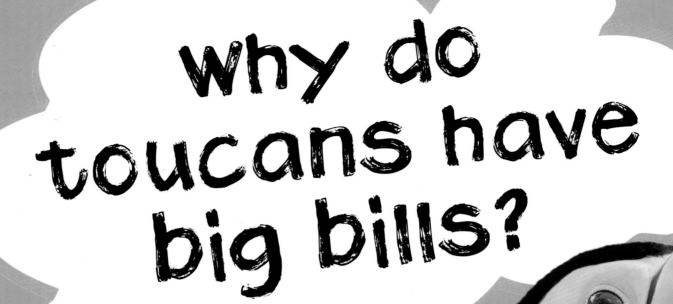

Toucans are birds with big, colourful bills (beaks). Both males and females have big bills, so they might be useful in attracting a mate. They may also help toucans reach and eat fruit high up in the trees.

Toucan

HOW big is a Goliath spider?

Goliath spiders are huge! They live in the rainforests of South America and can have a leg span of up to 30 centimetres. They eat insects and sometimes catch small birds to eat. Luckily, these spiders are harmless to people.

↗ Goliath spider

Make

Use a paper plate, pipe cleaners and tape to make a life-size model of a Goliath spider.

Does it rain every day in a rainforest?

It rains almost every day in a rainforest. This habitat is home to plants that need lots of rain and plenty of hot, sunny days. Without rain and warmth, rainforest plants cannot grow.

Yum yum!

Leeches are slug-like animals that live in rainforest rivers. They love to suck blood from animals and humans!

HOW slow is a sloth?

Sloths are possibly the slowest animals alive. They are so slow, it is almost impossible to see one moving. Sloths hang upside down in trees. Once a week, they slowly climb to the ground to poo. It takes them one minute to walk 2 metres!

Mother and baby sloth

Does chocolate grow on trees?

No, chocolate doesn't grow on trees, but the beans we use to make chocolate do. They are called cacao beans, and they grow in big pods on cacao trees.

Cacao pods

Why do monkeys howl?

Scratch and sniff!

Tapirs use their long snouts to sniff for food. They scratch around in mud to find berries and fruit.

Monkeys are very noisy animals. They live in groups, and need to howl, chatter and hoot to talk to one another. Howler monkeys live in South American jungles. They are some of the loudest animals in the world.

Go slow

Pretend to be a sloth. Measure 2 metres and see how slowly you can walk that distance.

which jungle cat has spots?

Jaguars are spotty jungle cats. Spots and stripes help animals to hide. Jaguars live in jungles and hide in trees and bushes. When they see or hear an animal they jump out and attack. Using colours and patterns to blend in is called camouflage.

Jaguar

Hide
Wear clothes that are a similar colour or pattern to your surroundings. How well hidden are you?

can lizards change colour?

Chameleons are lizards that can change colour. They may turn pink, red, green, blue, brown, yellow or even purple. Chameleons change colour when they are angry, or excited. They can also become the same colour as their surroundings.

Slime time!

Pitcher plants are bug-eating plants. Flies fall inside them, and get trapped in pools of liquid. The plants have slimy walls to stop flies escaping.

Rafflesia flower

what is the biggest flower?

The biggest flower is called rafflesia, and one bloom can grow to 90 centimetres wide — as wide as a table. Rafflesia flowers have thick, red petals and have a strong, bad smell that attracts insects to them.

which beetle is a giant?

Most beetles are smaller than a fingernail, but one is longer than your hand. It is a Hercules beetle, and males can grow to 19 centimetres long. They have long horns on their heads, which they use to fight each other.

Hercules beetle

who has the strongest teeth in the jungle?

Agoutis have such strong teeth they can bite through hard nut shells. Few animals are able to open the tough shells of Brazil nuts. Agoutis can bite through them to eat the tasty nut inside.

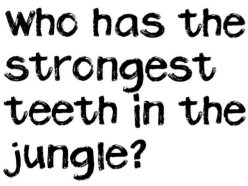
Agouti

Big bird!

A cassowary is a bird, but it cannot fly. Cassowaries have sharp claws on their feet, and they kick out if they're scared by intruders.

Count

If an agouti eats five nuts every day, how many will it eat in two days?

can a piranha eat a horse?

No, a single piranha can't eat a horse, but a group, or shoal, could. Piranhas are fierce fish that live in some rainforest rivers, and they have very sharp teeth. When a group of piranhas attack, they can eat a big animal in minutes.

Do kangaroos live in trees?

Kangaroos don't live in trees – unless they're tree kangaroos! The furry tree kangaroo is small enough to climb trees and walk along branches. It sleeps in the day and feeds on leaves and flowers at night.

Tree kangaroo

what is a bird of paradise?

Birds of paradise are some of the most beautiful birds in the world. The males have fine feathers in many colours. Some birds grow long tail feathers. They show off their feathers to females when it is time to mate.

King bird of paradise

Raggiana bird of paradise

Princess Stephana's bird of paradise

Good-looking!

Quetzals are colourful jungle birds. Males grow long tail feathers that can reach one metre in length!

Draw

Draw a bird of paradise and decorate it using pens, glue and scraps of brightly coloured paper.

HOW do lizards fly?

Lizards cannot really fly because they don't have wings, but some lizards can glide. They have flaps of skin that they stretch out to glide through the air when they leap from a tree.

what is the biggest butterfly?

Millions of butterflies and moths flutter through the world's rainforests. One of the biggest is Queen Alexandra's birdwing butterfly. It can measure nearly 30 centimetres from wing tip to wing tip.

↗

Queen Alexandra's birdwing butterfly

Why are jungle frogs so deadly?

Not all jungle frogs are deadly, but some have poisonous skin. Most poison-arrow frogs are small, and have colourful skin that is coated with poison. The golden poison-arrow frog is one of the deadliest of all, but it is no bigger than your thumb.

Golden poison-arrow frog

sweet bird!

Hummingbirds feed on the sweet juice made by flowers. When they hover at a flower, their wings make a humming sound.

Who eats all the leaves?

The floor of the forest is covered with dead leaves. Some of them will rot away. Others will be eaten by the billions of tiny animals that live in a jungle – such as ants, caterpillars, slugs and snails.

Find

Look under plants and stones to see garden animals, such as ants, beetles, and woodlice. Try not to disturb them.

Do lemurs wear rings on their tails?

No, lemurs do not wear rings on their tails! Ring-tailed lemurs have bands of black-and-white fur on their tails, which look like rings. When they walk, the lemurs wave their long furry tails in the air.

Ring-tailed lemur

Research
Using the Internet, find out the name of the island that lemurs live on. What other animals live there?

who is as thin as a pencil?

A baby vine snake is as thin as a pencil. An adult vine snake is about as thin as a grown-up's finger. Vine snakes live in trees and hunt birds and lizards to eat.

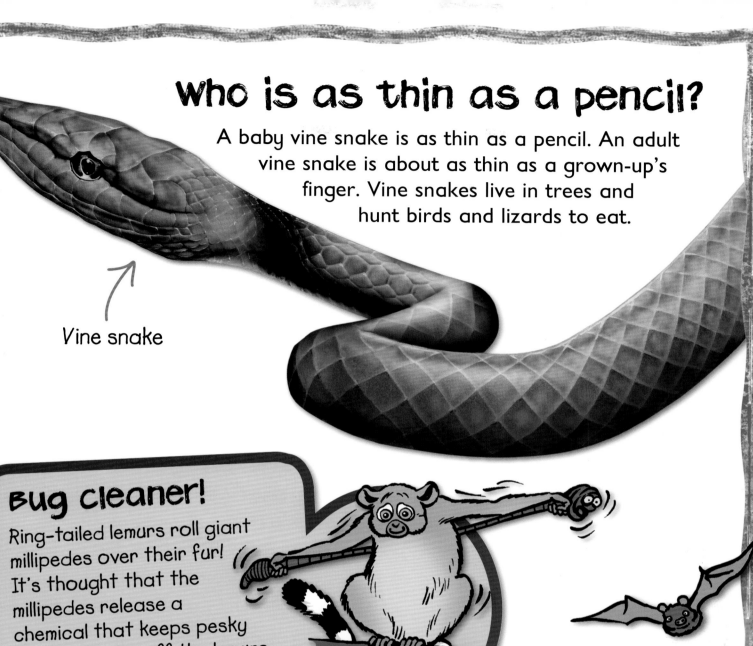

Vine snake

Bug cleaner!

Ring-tailed lemurs roll giant millipedes over their fur! It's thought that the millipedes release a chemical that keeps pesky flies and bugs off the lemurs.

why don't bats bump into trees?

Most jungle bats fly at the night. They don't bump into trees because they have a special sense that helps them to work out where things are, even in the dark. It is called echolocation.

Are there dragons in the jungle?

There are no real dragons in the jungle, but there are lizards that look like dragons! Boyd's dragon is an iguana that has a flap of skin under its chin, called a dewlap. It also has a row of spines that run along its back.

Boyd's → dragon

when is a leaf not a leaf?

When it is a leaf insect! Some rainforest insects pretend to be leaves or sticks. This means they can stay still and hide from birds and lizards that want to eat them. They also hide from other bugs they want to catch.

Leaf insect

Freeze

Lie on the floor like a leaf insect and stay still for as long as you can.

yummy honey!

Sun bears have very strong claws for digging into bees' nests. They lick out the honey with their long tongues.

which bugs light up the night?

Glow insects do. Some of these bugs are called glow-worms and others are called fireflies. Hundreds of them gather in a tree, and twinkle like Christmas lights, or stars in the sky.

who lives in the clouds?

Gorillas live in cloud forests, where the tops of the trees are covered in mist and cloud. These rainforests are often wet and cool, but gorillas don't mind. They have thick fur, and spend most of the day eating leaves, playing and sleeping.

Baby gorilla

Red-eyed
tree frogs

which frog has scary eyes?

Red-eyed tree frogs use their big red eyes to scare enemies. If disturbed, the frogs flash their bulging eyes. This may startle predators and scare them away.

Find it

Use an atlas or the Internet to find the Amazon River in the Amazon rainforest. It's in South America.

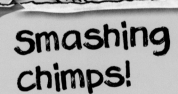

smashing chimps!

Clever chimps use stones as tools to crack open tough nuts and fruits.

why do animals move home?

When part of a rainforest dies, or is cut down, the animals that live there move to find a new place to live. Every year, many animals lose their homes when people cut down trees in rainforests.

why are tigers stripy?

Stripes may help tigers to hide while they hunt. It is difficult to spot a striped animal hiding in the shadows. Tigers often crouch in long grass waiting for an animal to pass by. Then they pounce!

Tiger

can apes be orange?

Some apes are orange! Orang-utans are large apes that live in jungles in Asia. Their fur is long, and orange-brown. Baby orang-utans stay with their mothers until they are about 8 years old.

Mother and baby orang-utan

Think

Orang-utans are apes. Can you think of any other types of ape?

Giant frog!

Goliath frogs live in jungle rivers and lakes, and are big enough to swallow lizards. They can be more than 30 centimetres long!

Do all birds live in trees?

Most birds live in trees, where they are safe from other animals. But some, such as the junglefowl, spend a lot of time on the ground. They find bugs, seeds and worms to eat there.

Which bird is Lord of the Jungle?

The Philippine eagle is called the 'Lord of the Jungle'. It is one of the biggest birds in the world. This eagle has huge talons (claws) and a strong, curved bill. It hunts other birds, snakes, wild cats, lemurs and even monkeys.

Flying lemur

Philippine eagle

when is a toad like a leaf?

When it is hidden on the forest floor! Some jungle frogs and toads have colours and patterns that help them to hide on trees, leaves or branches. The leaflitter toad has brown camouflage that makes it look like a dead leaf.

Leaflitter toad

Tongue-twister!

Okapis have very long tongues. They are so long, an okapi can use its tongue to lick its eyeballs clean!

why are some animals rare?

When the number of a species (type) of animal falls, it is said to be rare. Tigers, orang-utans and gorillas are rare. Animals become rare when they cannot find enough food, or their home in the wild has gone.

Think

Make up a story about three jungle animals and an adventure they have.

Why does a snake squeeze its food?

So it can eat it! The emerald tree boa is a rainforest snake. Once it has grabbed its prey, it wraps its body around it and squeezes it to death. This snake can grow to 2 metres long.

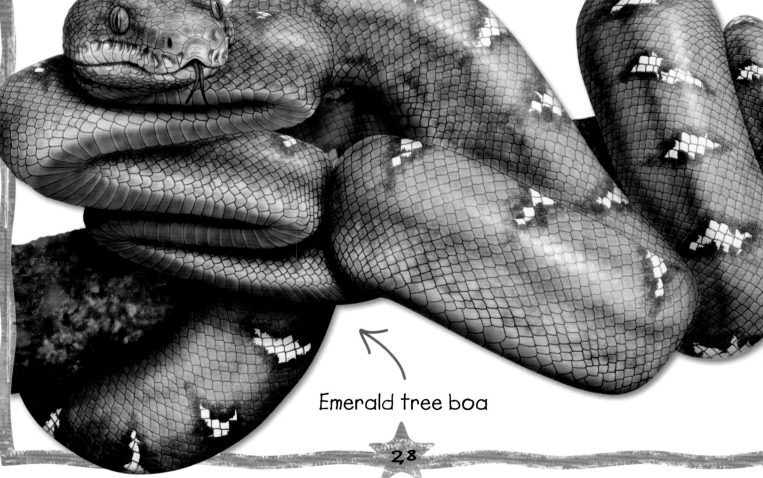

Emerald tree boa

Forest elephants

who has the biggest teeth in the jungle?

Elephants have the biggest teeth, called tusks. African forest elephants have tusks that point down, so they can walk through plants and trees without getting their tusks tangled in leaves!

sticky toes!

Gecko lizards are able to crawl on rocks and trees because they have sticky toes. Tiny hairs on their toes work like glue, to make them stick.

Do monkeys have beards?

Mangabey monkeys have tufts of white hair that look like beards! These may help the monkeys to communicate. Mangabeys live in the Africa, in groups called 'troops'.

Quiz time

Do you remember what you have read about rainforests? Here are some questions to test your memory. The pictures will help you. If you get stuck, read the pages again.

page 9

3. Does chocolate grow on trees?

page 12

4. Which beetle is a giant?

1. Which lizard can bark?

page 5

5. What is a bird of paradise?

page 15

2. How big is a Goliath spider?

page 7

6. Why are jungle frogs so deadly?

page 17

page 19

page 26

7. who is as thin as a pencil?

11. which bird is Lord of the jungle?

page 21

12. why are some animals rare?

page 27

8. when is a leaf not a leaf?

page 28

9. why do animals move home?

page 23

13. why does a snake squeeze its food?

10. Do all birds live in trees?

page 25

Answers

1. The tokay gecko
2. They have a leg span of 30 centimetres
3. No, but cacao beans do, and these are used to make chocolate
4. The Hercules beetle
5. A beautiful bird with bright feathers and a long tail
6. Because some have poisonous skin
7. The vine snake
8. When it's a leaf insect
9. Because their rainforest homes are cut down
10. Because the rainforest is being cut down
11. The Phillipine eagle
12. Because they don't have enough food or their homes have disappeared
13. So it can eat it

Index